WILLIAM SHAKESPEARE

A Life From Beginning to End

Copyright © 2017 by Hourly History.

Table of Contents

Introduction

William Shakespeare is quite possibly one of the most famous historical figures of all time. His theatrical body of work is performed more often than any other playwright in history, and his plays have been translated into every major language. He is considered the greatest writer in the English language and the paramount dramatist of all time. These accolades are not without their deserved merit, and a close look at his life proves they are well-earned.

Shakespeare lived in England during the rule of Queen Elizabeth I, commonly referred to as the Elizabethan Era. This was an intriguing time in England, both politically and artistically. Religious tensions between Catholics and Protestants were high, the nation was on edge as war loomed with mainland Europe, and Elizabethan dissenters plotted to take the throne. Ireland would rebel against English rule, and the black plague would strike at the heart of London. The death of Elizabeth I changed the world in which Shakespeare lived, and brought many of these events to a head. Guy Fawkes and his famous Gunpowder Plot would shock the nation, and a mass panic would result in witch trials throughout the nation.

Despite such political and religious stressors, Shakespeare's world was constantly growing and changing. Medical and physical sciences would announce amazing discoveries, intrepid explorers would map previously uncharted parts of the world and return with tales of untold wonders. It is these magnificent discoveries that fueled the creative collaboration that took place in London during Shakespeare's life and afforded him the inspiration to experiment with form and style, as well as provided him with endless material for intricate plots and rich, three-dimensional characters. William Shakespeare was born into a world that granted him the tools to change the face of artistic expression for humanity and made his life story worthy of telling and re-telling for the rest of time.

Chapter One

A Legend is Born

"I say there is no darkness but ignorance."

—William Shakespeare, Twelfth Night

A modern imagining of Elizabethan England often conjures two conflicting images: One of colorfully gritty life in central London, where the lower-class of the city were packed together in noisy and unsanitary conditions, struggling to survive in a world that had not yet seen many modern advances in technology, automation, and convenience. Conversely, a present-day idea may include the romanticized view of English aristocracy under the traditional monarchy—rich fabrics, expensive and extravagant gowns, high-brow political intrigues and forbidden romances. Neither of these highly romanticized interpretations, however, accurately depict what life was like in Elizabethan England as a whole.

Life outside of London moved at a significantly slower pace. London was one of the first urban centers in the United Kingdom, and the further one lived from the capital, the quicker one entered a country that was defined by rural living. The excitement and fast pace of urban life would quickly dissipate, and most of the population of England in that period were far removed from both the cultural and political goings-on at the country's heart. Travel at the time was expensive, difficult, and dangerous. Many Englishmen and women lived and died without traveling more than a half day's journey from the village in which they were born. Rural communities were small and tight-knit, with many generations of the same family occupying the same house for centuries. There would have been little opportunities to climb the socio-economic ladder, and so rural villages functioned as a sort of microcosm, much separated from the fast-paced activity and rich diversity of any urban center.

It is in such a rural village that William Shakespeare was born, and spent much of his early life. Shakespeare was born in the hamlet of Stratford-upon-Avon, over 100 miles northwest of London. He was born into a middle-class family in April 1564, the son of John Shakespeare and Mary Arden. His baptismal record with the Church of England stated he was baptized on April 26, but does not list a date of birth. The custom of the period was to wait three days after the birth of a child before baptism, and therefore his date of birth is listed by most historians as April 23, 1564. This holds a significant degree of poetry for many historians, as William Shakespeare would die on the same date in 1616.

William's father John was a successful glove-maker, held a seat on his local city council, and would be elected as mayor of Stratford when William was four years old. William's mother Mary was the daughter of a wealthy landowner who lived in the area. Mary would give birth to eight children, five of whom reached adulthood. William was the third-born and the eldest son. This put young William in a place of significant privilege and advantage for the time period—as the son of a rural, middle-class family, he wanted for very little. His hometown of Stratford was rare overall: in spite of being very small (with a survey from around the same time listing only 217 houses) it was a hub for the raising of sheep and harvesting of wool, which was often processed and sent to London directly from Stratford.

The rural way of life that was characterized by isolation and stasis gradually began to change in the Elizabethan Era. Political and religious tensions were at an all-time high, and with potential war on the horizon, certain English-produced goods came into high demand. The middle class formed for the first time and the population of rural communities profited the most from this economic bounty. Wars already underway elsewhere in mainland Europe brought refugees to Britain, where they flocked to the countryside to ply their trades. Insular villages saw new traffic pass through on the roadways, and immigrants joined their ranks for the first time. Many people in rural England had their first encounters with people who spoke other languages or had different colored skin. A good number of these immigrants were literate and well-educated, disseminating their knowledge of literature, math, and science into under-served communities with no access to higher educational services. Rural towns and villages within England did not have the means to see the world—so instead, the world came to them.

These changes affected Stratford, especially economically. The main trade of sheep and their wool products would have been in high demand in the political climate of pre-war readiness, and Stratford would have benefitted from the booming demand. This increase in the overall wealth of Stratford (and William's own family) may have contributed to his early education. The local grammar school, King's New School, had been built in 1553 and was located only a quarter of a mile from William's home. While the quality of education in schools across England could differ wildly, it was likely that the relative financial comfort in the area allowed most children to attend school through their 14th year. Laws set forth by royal decree dictated that Latin text be taught in all grammar schools throughout the United Kingdom, and a huge part of William's early education would have had its foundation in classical Latin authors. This no doubt contributed to his literacy and remarkable use of language in his writing in adulthood, while his upbringing in a rural area with no particularly advanced education allowed him to connect on an emotional level to the "common man."

Chapter Two

The Lost Years

"No sooner met but they looked; no sooner looked but they loved; no sooner loved but they sighed; no sooner sighed but they asked one another the reason; no sooner knew the reason but they sought the remedy; and in these degrees have they made a pair of stairs to marriage."

—William Shakespeare, As You Like It

On November 27, 1582, at the age of 18, William Shakespeare married 26-year-old Anne Hathaway. The wedding took place in a much shorter time frame than was typical for the period, as the church official had granted them an exception from certain standard procedures. The following day, neighbors of Hathaway signed a legally binding oath under penalty of fine, declaring their guarantee that there were no legal impediments to the marriage. Six months later, Anne gave birth to their first child: a daughter, Susanna.

These facts form nearly the complete extent of information that is known about William Shakespeare's wife, but the unusual circumstances under which they were married have raised speculation and theory for centuries. The age difference between William and Anne has been made a point of scandal by many modern historians, though a thorough review of marriage records for that period reveal it was not unusual for a wife to be older than her husband. Eldest daughters, as Anne Hathaway would have been, would often take on the role of raising any younger siblings, delaying the age at which they would marry and start their own homes. The fact of Susanna's birth only six months after the marriage took place, as well as the legal declarations of Anne's neighbors, have also been dramatized in the present day. Antenuptial pregnancies were extremely common in rural areas of England, and the actual acquisition of the marriage license would merely be a formality for the purposes of the Church of England.

However, the spinning of this information in sensational ways pervades, especially when very little else is known about the finer details of William and Anne's married life. Two years after Susanna's birth in 1583, Anne gave birth again, this time to fraternal twins, Judith and Hamnet. Hamnet died in 1596 at the age of 11 after a minor resurgence of the bubonic plague. By this time, William had been living in London for over four years, while his family remained in Stratford.

It is after the birth of Judith and Hamnet in 1585 that history loses track of William Shakespeare, and he is not discovered in any civil or legal document until 1592, by which time several of his plays were already being produced and performed on London stages. These lost years, along with the mysterious vacuum of information about his relationship with his wife and children, leave much to be speculated.

Books and films based on Shakespeare's life have often explained his departure to London as a way for him to escape a loveless marriage. Depictions of his early life in storytelling media have used the evidence of Anne's early pregnancy to suggest she became pregnant on purpose, as a form of entrapment. Even ignoring the fact that such circumstances were not scandalous, and in fact normal, Anne came from a relatively wealthy family herself. Her motive would not likely be for financial gain or an improvement in social status. There would be little reason to believe that it was not William's intention to marry Anne when their courtship first began, with the pregnancy merely providing an opportunity to make the courtship permanent and official.

Others have depicted the relationship as supportive yet tempestuous. This may well be the most likely theory that has survived among modern scholars. In Shakespeare's will, he bequeaths Anne the home's "second-best bed." Many among the academic community have viewed this as a slight, that perhaps William was suggesting in a very pointed way that she was second-best in his life. However, in Elizabethan culture, the "best bed" in the house was commonly reserved only for guests. The "second-best" bed in the home was almost certainly the marital bed, meaning such a bequest would have been symbolic of their relationship and held much meaning for his widow. Anne, in her later years, was open about her desire to be interred next to her husband, leading many to believe their relationship was loving despite the physical distance between them for most of their married life. The lost years have given many modern storytellers the artistic license to fill in the gap in a variety of ways, while the truth of the matter is lost to time.

Despite these blank pages in William's history, it has been reliably documented that he returned to Stratford for some period at least once every year, and upon his retirement from writing and the London theatre, he returned to Stratford to be with his wife and grown children, rather than remain in the city. These minor details suggest perhaps his relationship with his wife was not as oppressive or forced as some historians have claimed. These lost years have been a subject of speculation, debate, and contention within the scholarly community since as early as the dawn of the twentieth century. They can be added to the list of controversies surrounding William's life, littered among arguments regarding his religion, sexuality, and political beliefs.

Chapter Three

Early Career

"[He] supposes he is as well able to bombast out a blank verse as the best of you."

—Robert Greene

The details of William Shakespeare's departure from Stratford, arrival in London, and the writing and staging of his earliest plays are all swept away within his lost years. From the first documented account of his presence in London, however, it is easy to discern that he had gained quite the reputation for himself among the artistic and theatrical community. In 1592, playwright Robert Greene published an attack on William Shakespeare's work in a widely distributed pamphlet. Green was a member of an elite group of playwrights well established in London by this time, the most famous among them being Christopher Marlowe. This loose group of men has been named posthumously by modern historians as the "university wits," as all of them had come from high-brow private educations at such institutions as Oxford and Cambridge.

Greene's attack on Shakespeare boiled down to the fact that Shakespeare was, in a sense, reaching beyond his station. His plays strove to be lofty and high-brow, while

Shakespeare himself had no formal advanced education, in stark opposition to Greene and his compatriots. He accused Shakespeare of recycling and dressing up old ideas and themes, rather than establishing new and unique stories such as those that were put together by more educated writers. Shakespeare, in a few short years, had gained the attention of a well-established, highly educated, and successful playwright in the London theatre scene. Educated or not, Shakespeare must have posed enough of a threat by 1592 to warrant such an aggressive attack on his work and character.

William Shakespeare, as well as his fellow writers of the university wits, were responsible for two very different branches of artistic and political expression in the London theatre during the Elizabethan Era. While the likes of Robert Greene would likely be loath to admit it, the educated secular playwrights of that time gave rise to the opportunity of the common man to have his writing seen and his plays staged within the English popular theatre. Dominating European theatre at this time were medieval-era miracle plays. These were essentially morality plays based heavily on biblical allegories, with very little room for experimentation or interpretation. The religious tensions of that century between Catholics and the newly-established Protestants may have been the beginnings of the death of the medieval religious drama, while university educated writers steered public discourse toward more secular themes. In turn, less educated writers would have made these secular subjects more relatable and accessible to the common man living in London, who formed the bulk of the audience at that time.

Historians have struggled to form a cohesive timeline of Shakespeare's early years in London. Most estimates place his work onstage for the first time anywhere from the mid-1580s to just before Greene published his scathing opinion piece in 1592. To place his early success as late as 1592, however, condenses a large body of his written and produced work into an extremely short period of time. By the end of the 1590s, Shakespeare would be massively wealthy, his name would have been common knowledge across all of London, and the words "William Shakespeare" underneath the title of any published text would have guaranteed second and third printings would be required to keep up with demand. If Shakespeare only began producing and staging his plays in 1592, this rise to fame would have been unprecedented and occurred nearly overnight.

Regardless, by 1594 he was popular enough among the common theatre-going populace that he was commissioned by the theatre group Lord Chamberlain's Men to be a sort of resident playwright. From then on, Shakespeare's plays were performed only by this theatre troupe, in which Shakespeare himself would eventually gain part ownership. It wasn't long before Lord Chamberlain's Men were the most popular group of players in the entire city, though this can hardly be attributed solely to Shakespeare's works. The acting troupe was backed by several extremely wealthy financiers, and their leader, Richard Burbage, was lauded both as a savvy businessman and an excellent actor. Combined with the unique material Shakespeare was producing, they would have been unstoppable. After Queen Elizabeth I's death in 1603, the group was held in such high esteem that King James I became their sole patron.

Shakespeare's plays did pop up in other venues throughout his career, though they were probably staged without the knowledge or consent of Lord Chamberlain's Men. The London theatre scene was highly competitive and extremely cutthroat. Inter-troupe espionage was not unheard of, with actors entering other theatres attempting to steal scripts. Since access to printing presses was difficult (and expensive), scripts were often handwritten for each individual part, containing only the actor's own lines, as well as a word or two of the previous "cue" line. This meant that any script that was stolen or pilfered would only contain a tiny fraction of the overall dialogue of the play. Unless the script was for a leading role, it would be of very little use in discerning plot, theme, staging, or anything other than a sense of the playwright's writing style. Another method of play theft involved paying to attend a performance and later jotting down plot points or lines of dialogue that could be recalled. Such bootleg productions would have drawn theatre-goers based on title and false attribution of authorship alone, though the actual script of the stolen play probably did not even closely resemble the original product except in terms of general plot points.

While Shakespeare's stratospheric rise to success is evident (by 1597, the company had made Shakespeare so wealthy that he bought the second-largest house in Stratford, as well as purchasing a large portion of shares of the Stratford tithe), there is difficulty in dating and placing which of his plays were the earliest and gained the most popularity. These details, if obtained, could lend themselves to revealing even more of Shakespeare's inner life, as the evolution of his writing could be more closely traced.

Chapter Four

The First Plays

"So wise so young, they say, do never live long."

—William Shakespeare, Richard III

Robert Greene's pamphlet in 1592, in which Shakespeare is mentioned in London for the first time, directly quotes a link from *Henry VI Part III*. By this time, then, the *Henry VI* trilogy was already written and in the public sphere of London theatre, and historians can attribute these historical plays to his earlier canon of work, thus forming the basis of the often-debated timeline of Shakespeare's works. There is also documentation that *Richard III* was being performed during this period. Shakespeare in his early years, then, focused largely on historically based plays, which was a trend in theatre at that time. Other playwrights (including Robert Greene and Christopher Marlowe) were also writing royal historical plays concurrently. All writers seemed to draw their primary inspiration from Raphael Holinshed's book *Chronicles of England, Ireland, and Scotland*. Historically derived material was a popular subject among the general populace, so playhouses may have been filling their stages with these types of plays to meet demand, increase business, and compete effectively with rival acting troupes and theatres.

Though to this day there is no concrete evidence of Shakespeare's other early work, based on such details as handling of primary and secondary plot, character development, treatment of women and minorities, as well as overall mastery of verse, grammar, vocabulary, and syntax, scholars have educated guesses on what his other earliest plays might have been. There has been an overall consensus in recent years that his very first completed play (though not necessarily the first staged) was *Titus Andronicus*, followed by *The Comedy of Errors*, *Taming of the Shrew*, and *Two Gentlemen of Verona*. Overall, historians and Shakespearean scholars seem to agree that these works are "rougher" in their composition. While *Titus Andronicus* and *Taming of the Shrew* are still among his most produced plays, they are highly criticised in theatrical circles for many reasons. *Titus Andronicus* does not deal well with introducing and neatly closing secondary and tertiary plots, and the play abandons many loose threads while managing to be extremely violent (a subject of great spectacle and entertainment for the people of Elizabethan London, though not dealt with in the play with any particular finesse). *Taming of the Shrew* is highly criticized as well for the sexist nature of the work, even for the era in which it was written. Scholars agree this was likely among his very early plays due to the fact that the female roles (and the treatment of female characters) in his later plays shift dramatically toward empowered women that are regarded in a largely positive light, as opposed to the harshly negative and condescending tone of *Taming of the Shrew*.

Shakespeare's early histories, however, share a common theme of weak and corrupt rulers and the catastrophic aftermath of ineffectual rule. Some scholars have attributed this as a support of the currently reigning Tudor dynasty, while others have interpreted these productions as a political statement that functioned as a subtle warning. Elizabeth I's father was Henry VIII, infamous throughout history for his break from the Catholic Church in Rome and the founding of the Church of England. His formation of the Protestant faith allowed him to divorce and re-marry, a request which the Roman Catholic Pope had denied him. Upon Henry's death, Mary Tudor, Henry's daughter from his first Catholic marriage, assumed the throne and attempted to overthrow her father's church and re-instate Catholicism as the country's primary religion. Her relentless pursuit and execution of defiant Protestants as heretics earned her the name "Bloody Mary." Upon her early death (likely due to uterine cancer), the only legitimate heir to the throne was Elizabeth, the child of Henry and his second wife, Anne Boleyn. Elizabeth, who had been ostracized from royal life for most of her youth, wanted to rule based on "peace and good counsel." While she embraced the Protestant faith, she was much less zealous than both her father and her half-sister and was often seen to be carrying Catholic symbols of faith.

Based on her advice, the Parliament repealed all heresy laws but made attendance at Protestant mass and the use of the Protestant-based *Book of Common Prayer* compulsory across the United Kingdom. Therefore, while a Catholic no longer risked burning at the stake, there were steep consequences to practicing openly, and many Catholics hid their faith from their communities for fear of retribution.

These political intricacies surrounding religion may have influenced much of Shakespeare's work, but particularly his choice of subject matter in his early plays. Historians who argue the earlier histories were an attempt to declare solidarity with the Elizabethan dynasty base this on the assumption that William Shakespeare was a practicing Protestant. Those who see his thematic choices as opposition, however, have opened the floor to the possibility that William Shakespeare may have been a secret Catholic.

Shakespeare's religious practices have been another bone of contention among scholars for several centuries. William's mother Mary Arden had come from a family that was primarily Catholic, though she herself was not, which only increased confusion surrounding the issue. Irish academic Edmond Malone, the most respected Shakespearean scholar of his day, was sure he would settle the debate in the eighteenth century when he found a document hidden in the rafters of Shakespeare's childhood home. The document bore the signature of John Shakespeare, William's father, and attested that John would remain a Catholic "in his heart," despite attending Protestant churches as the law required. Malone had been shown the document and described it in one of his books, but the original was subsequently lost, and Malone's description came under debate. However, in the 1980s, a document nearly identical in form and composition surfaced. Though it was signed by another person, Malone had described the until now unknown text in great detail, and modern scholars largely agree that the pledge signed by John Shakespeare was likely genuine.

William's father, then, was secretly a practicing Catholic, which casts into doubt the playwright's own religious beliefs. Being baptized into the Protestant faith is not a guarantee of where an individual's loyalties or beliefs may lie, especially if one's true faith is actively oppressed by the ruling powers. Similarly, a devout pledge of faith by William's father does not necessarily mean William followed in his father's footsteps. The document, then, has made the subject even more of a grey area in recent years, rather than shedding light on the mystery.

There exist, therefore, two opposing camps of academics regarding Shakespeare's focus on these particular points in history. Any possible message or goal is obscured behind the mystery of his motivation, though his religious views may not be a factor at all. The histories were popular among audiences of the day—Christopher Marlowe was writing very similar material at the same time, also using Holinshed's book as a source. Shakespeare, in choosing his early body of work, may have simply been giving the people what they wanted.

Chapter Five

The Evolution of William Shakespeare

"If you prick us, do we not bleed? If you tickle us, do we not laugh? If you poison us, do we not die? And if you wrong us, shall we not revenge?"

—William Shakespeare, The Merchant of Venice

By the mid-1590s, William Shakespeare's work shifted focus, and he produced many of his most popular romantic comedies, which included *A Midsummer Night's Dream, Much Ado About Nothing*, and *As You Like It*. But this period was not solely focused on light-hearted stories where the heroes and heroines ended up happily ever after—it is bookended by two of Shakespeare's early tragedies: *Romeo and Juliet* marked the beginning of this productive middle period, while the tragedy *Julius Caesar* effectively marked the end.

Many of Shakespeare's earliest plays that were not explicit histories were largely based on a popular form of Italian theatre in that period, namely *commedia dell'arte*. This theatrical form was characterized by a rigid cast of characters that were the personification of a single human stereotype, such as the clown, the maid, the lover, and the letch. It often involved the tight execution of physical comedy gags and was highly stylized in movement and staging. Shakespeare may indeed have been guilty of Robert Greene's criticism of re-using established material, merely anglicizing certain characteristics to make them more relatable to a common and less educated audience.

Shakespeare's middle years saw him shed this amateur practice and venture into new territory, where he began to experiment with original plots based on universal themes of love, magic, and the first signs of Shakespeare's mythically enduring powerhouse: the flawed tragic hero. His finesse in contrasting comedic scenes with more serious ones adds depth to his comedies; a genre which, at the time, was centered on one-note stock characters with sparse details of life outside of scenes in which they were required.

Shakespeare began to play with class and race in unique ways for the period, often pushing characters from different socio-economic strata together for both comedic and philosophical effect. His portrayal of Shylock, the Jewish moneylender in *The Merchant of Venice,* may seem derogatory and insulting to modern audiences but portrayed a Jewish character in greater depth and with more empathy than any documented portrayal before. Shylock's famous monologue at the crescendo of the play sought to compare Jews and Christians in purely human terms. This may have been an effort to make a Jewish character, who would immediately be vilified by a Christian audience, more relatable. No writer, philosopher, or playwright had posed such a comparison or question to a common audience before.

It was also unconventional for the time for a playwright to mix such disparate genres and styles as magic and realism. *A Midsummer Night's Dream*, while being a light-hearted comedy focusing on two romantically intertwined couples, is driven largely by the mischief of fairies and their magic. This use of magic for magic's sake would not have been commonly seen in theatre at that time, coming from the tail end of a highly religious and faith-based theatrical practice in the medieval era. Later, Shakespeare would take this genre-mixing even further in what many academics refer to as his "problem plays"—*Cymbeline, The Tempest,* and *A Winter's Tale* among them. Within these particular plays, Shakespeare moved with deft precipitousness from classic comedic scenes to poignant tragedy, often concluding these plots with a happy ending in which the main heroes find forgiveness for their flaws and errors.

Romeo and Juliet was particularly unique in this time because romance was not generally an acceptable storyline for use in tragedies of the day. In fact, if one were to see the play staged or read it for the first time without any intimate knowledge of its plot structure, the first half of the play would seem to be a comedy. It is not until the death of Romeo's friend Mercutio in Act III that the audience is surprised to learn they are indeed watching a play that will end tragically. This reversal of expectations may have been thrilling to audiences of the period, who were watching theatrical convention evolve before their very eyes.

The definitive final play of this period, *Julius Caesar*, has typically marked Shakespeare's arrival at peak poetic form. In 2005, Shakespearean scholar James Shapiro would allude to it as an almost self-aware piece of theatre, managing to weave ancient politics with contemporary issues of the day, create rich and empathetic characters, and explore broader themes that may even relate to Shakespeare's writing as a whole body of work in itself.

His work in these mid-years has been examined closely because so little information about his private life remains. History must draw from his published body of work any social, political, or personal views he held, and can only speculate on his change and growth over his time in London. The bulk of a cohesive analysis of Shakespeare's life must be done through the lens of the writing he left behind, the study of which is subjective and by no means definitive. Interpretations of Shakespeare's personality and opinions have shifted dramatically in the centuries since he lived, and will likely continue to do so in the centuries to come. In this sense, William Shakespeare takes on a mythical, legendary quality as his life is interpreted through the fiction he created.

This output of plays in Shakespeare's learning years and their specific chronology have allowed scholars to study the evolution of Shakespeare's style, as well as his poetic form and grasp of language. History has viewed this time in Shakespeare's life as a period of extreme growth in how he addressed character particularity, which paved the way for the deeply human and flawed three-dimensional tragic heroes he would write about in his final years in London.

Chapter Six

The Golden Years

"Fortune brings in some boats that are not steered."

—William Shakespeare, Cymbeline

It is in the early 1600s that Shakespeare really hit his stride and peaked as a writer and artist. There is very little disagreement amongst scholars regarding this period—it was easily his most productive and advanced. Lord Chamberlain's Men had become so successful that by 1599, they had constructed a theatre on the Thames' south bank called the Globe. This was the first theatre ever built by actors specifically for actors, and many of Shakespeare's most famous tragedies were written to be performed within this space.

The beginning of the seventeenth century saw Shakespeare cast off the normal writing conventions of the period, which were evident in many of his earlier works. He continued a trend he had begun with *Romeo and Juliet*, using romance as a plot point within tragedies. This was not an accepted practice in the Elizabethan Era, and Shakespeare was the first to explore romantic themes within the confines of a tragedy. The finest examples of these stories from his golden period would be *Othello* and *Macbeth*, both of which use sexual or romantic relationships in different ways to further drive the plot, provide motive or impetus for action, and fuel the tragic circumstances in their denouements.

Antony and Cleopatra and *Coriolanus* were penned during Shakespeare's most productive years, and have been considered by writers, poets, and scholars alike as some of Shakespeare's best use of verse, meter, and poetic imagery.

Hamlet was also written at this time, somewhere between 1599 and 1603, with staging specifically written for the Globe. It has endured as Shakespeare's most famous play as well as his longest. *Hamlet* has been counted as one of the most powerful and influential works of literature of all time and has been at the top of Shakespeare's list of most performed works since 1879. It would be remiss not to mention the connection between the titular character and the name of Shakespeare's only son, who had died of bubonic plague only a few years prior, at the age of 11. Some scholars have suggested that the play was written in direct response to Hamnet's death and became the powerhouse piece of literature that it did due to a father's grief. There is very little beyond the circumstantial connection of their names to give this theory any credence, but the similarity should be noted nonetheless.

It was within the confines of *Hamlet*'s structure that Shakespeare perfected his tragic hero. Shakespeare defined these uniquely human characters in his tragedies by placing among their noble and admirable traits an essential flaw. Scholars have viewed many of his tragic heroes as archetypes of hubris—that bad things will happen even to the best of people because it is within human nature for each person to have one disastrous trait they are powerless to change. For Hamlet, that flaw was indecision. His inability to make a choice regarding the retribution for his father's murder led to the deaths of nearly the entire cast of characters within the play.

In contrast, Shakespeare's other tragic heroes were undone by their hastiness, their need to act quickly before gathering a complete set of facts. Othello allowed the poisonous Iago to convince him of the infidelity of his wife and murdered her before her innocence could be discovered; Macbeth unwittingly fulfilled the prophecy of the witches by murdering Duncan, an action he thought would prevent the divination from coming to pass.

Othello, likely written around 1603, was a uniquely interesting choice of story to write in Shakespeare's time, since it dealt so intimately with race and sex. Othello is often portrayed as African in modern productions of the play, though he is referred primarily throughout the course of the play as a "Moor." In Elizabethan language, this may have indeed referred to a man of African descent, but more likely referred to someone of Middle Eastern origin. Othello, then, was a play that was about more than the "other" in terms of race—it was highly likely that Shakespeare intended to refer to Othello's religion, as well. Shakespeare would use clear language to differentiate Othello from his peers, particularly his ill-fated wife, Desdemona, whose pale skin is spoken of poetically several times throughout the play. Shakespeare also turned another old social convention on its head in this play, as several characters would remark that Desdemona was sexually voracious, to the point that it scared the much more hesitant and strait-laced Othello. These gender-swapped attitudes toward sex would be a plot device later in the play, but also may have been a social and political commentary on women's sexual rights in that period, particularly in the urban city of London where women's behaviour was much more closely scrutinized and codified than it would have been in the rural countryside.

The actor who played Othello, however, would most certainly not have been a man of color. In fact, a person of color would not take the stage as the titular character until 1833 by actor Ira Aldridge. While depictions of Moors would not be rare in Elizabethan playhouses, *Othello* would be the first time in the history of documented English theatre that a character of color would be the leading role in a play. Despite his racial and religious differences from the bulk of an Elizabethan audience, Othello is depicted as a fast-acting, hot-tempered hero, only brought to ruin by his scheming friend Iago.

Iago, on the other hand, is one of Shakespeare's finest examples of a villain—his monologues, which would have been spoken directly to the audience, are full of rich imagery and language that guide the theatre-goer through the psychological make-up of villainy. Such analytic detail to character and motivation had not been seen before. Most of Shakespeare's contemporaries would have been focused on conforming to plot and language conventions of a much stiffer style of theatre that was dominated by one-dimensional stock characters. It is easy to imagine an audience at *Othello* awed, confused and delighted by this new look at character all at once.

In 1603, James I had become Britain's new monarch, and King Chamberlain's Men were the most popular and successful theatre company in London. They won the attention of the king, who became their sole patron at this time. The company was renamed The King's Men, and records indicate they performed at least seven different plays at the royal court between 1604 and 1605. With such heavy financial backing, from 1608 forward, The King's Men were able to perform year-round by staging plays indoors at Blackfriars Theatre in the winter, and at the Globe in the summer.

Macbeth was written shortly after *Othello* and performed for the first time around 1606. This would have put Shakespeare's company well within the period of patronage of the king and widened their audience considerably. With *Macbeth* added to his canon of work, in a few short years Shakespeare would write plays that dealt with race, sex, the taboo supernatural, and politics. *Macbeth* has been viewed by academics as not only Shakespeare's best play but also his strongest and most obvious socio-political commentary. The connection of this evolution of themes within his work to the company's sudden spotlight within the royal court should not be ignored.

For the source material of the play, Shakespeare returned to Holinshed's *Chronicles of England, Scotland,*

and Ireland, basing names and locations on real historical events. The actual sequence of these events in the play, however, differ wildly from their real-world counterparts. In 1605, just a year before Shakespeare would pen the play, Guy Fawkes and his compatriots would attempt to assassinate King James I and blow up the Houses of Parliament in what history would call the Gunpowder Plot. The planned rebellion was in response to a lifetime of Catholic oppression in England; religious tensions and politics were responsible for fanning the flames of the failed plot. Guy Fawkes and eight of his co-conspirators were convicted and sentenced to be hanged.

Chief among those blamed for the Gunpowder Plot was Henry Garnet, the head of the Jesuit Church in England at that time. He too was executed for his complicity in the planned terrorist attack. While not a conspirator himself, he had forewarning of the planned rebellion, which had been revealed to him while he was hearing confession. Under his religious doctrine, Garnet was bound not to repeat what he heard within the confessional booth, and though the plot was foiled before lives were lost, Garnet was blamed for not warning the authorities.

The subsequent manhunt for Henry Garnet is eerily reminiscent of many of the scenes interspersed throughout *Macbeth* and is referenced outright by a minor character in one of the later points of the play. The trial of Fawkes, Garnet, and their allies would have been the main subject of discussion for months in central London, and with *Macbeth*, Shakespeare allowed himself for the first time to blatantly connect his work with contemporary correlating events in the real world.

Macbeth proves that Shakespeare was a much brighter tactician than perhaps modern academics give him credit—he managed to weave in contemporary politic themes that would be controversial to display or stage at court, but set those themes within a framework of history and legend, disguising what may have been an ulterior political motive.

Chapter Seven

Poetic Works

"Describe Adonis, and the counterfeit
Is poorly imitated after you;
On Helen's cheek all art of beauty set,
And you in Grecian tires are painted new."

—William Shakespeare, Sonnet LIII

William Shakespeare was not only a playwright, and over the course of his professional career in London, he wrote and compiled 154 sonnets, the contents of which have fueled the fires of further speculation into his private life.

Evidence had suggested that Shakespeare wrote these sonnets over the span of his career and only published them as a collection in 1609. The sonnets are typically grouped for printing based on the subject of each sonnet, but very few historians believe that this was the intended order Shakespeare meant for them to be arranged and doubt even further that they were written in a chronological order that follows their arrangement in publication.

Nevertheless, Shakespeare's sonnets seem to be addressed to two primary individuals and have been the center of the centuries-old mystery of Shakespeare's private life in London. Sonnets 1 through 126 are addressed to the Fair Youth—an astonishingly beautiful young man with whom the "poet" of the sonnets was obsessed. Since the nineteenth century, poets, academics, and historians alike have analyzed the Fair Youth sonnets in excruciating detail in an attempt to parse out information that may reflect back on William Shakespeare and his sexuality.

There exist two parts to any speculation based on sonnets 1 through 126: the first, was the love being described within these sonnets platonic or romantic? The second, was Shakespeare writing these sonnets using his own voice and perspective, or was Shakespeare using the character of another poet, and not referring to himself at all? The 200-year-old question has become: were the sonnets autobiographical?

The first 17 sonnets in the Fair Youth series were descriptions of the young man's nearly ineffable beauty. They urged him to marry and procreate as soon as possible, so that his physical form would not die with him, but rather he would create equally beautiful children. The tone of the sonnets took a dramatic turn, however, at sonnet 18, easily the most enduringly famous of Shakespeare's sonnets: "Shall I compare thee to a summer's day?" This poem is possibly the most often quoted piece of romantic writing today, so it would be difficult to argue against the overtly romantic nature of the poet's feelings toward the Fair Youth. The remainder of the poems in this series document the ups and downs of the poet's relationship with the young man and introduces the primary subject of sonnets 127 through 154: The Dark Lady.

The sonnets dedicated to an unnamed and married woman with black hair are overtly sexual within the structure of physical intimacy, in comparison to a more suggestive erotic romanticism within the sonnets dedicated to the Fair Youth. There are those that have used the distinction in handling of erotic material as evidence that the Fair Youth sonnets were concerned with platonic love, and the Dark Lady sonnets are about romantic love; the entire theme of the collection would be the comparing and contrasting of the two.

Several sonnets in the series, however, weave the lives of the three characters together, chief among them sonnet 144. This particular sonnet describes an affair between the Dark Lady and the Fair Youth, which leads the wounded poet or narrator to sever all ties with both figures. While this may have been merely a creative and intricate narrative that Shakespeare created to connect his poems and serve as a metaphor, many historians would disagree. They believe the sonnets are explicit re-tellings of events, relationships, and conflicts that Shakespeare experienced. Clara Longworth de Chambrun, a Shakespearean scholar who contributed much to discourse in the eighteenth century regarding the sonnets possible autobiographical nature, wrote, "None who hears the cry of remorse and anguish in Shakespeare's poems can doubt that their author traversed a period of great moral suffering."

The suggestion, then, from the collective body of 154 sonnets, if they are regarded as even partially autobiographical, is that Shakespeare was not strictly heterosexual. There are some, to be sure, that occupy the autobiographical camp and also view the Fair Youth poems as discussions on platonic love, but they comprise a small group. Very few scholars have suggested that Shakespeare was explicitly homosexual and instead choose the controversial middle ground that Shakespeare was bisexual.

The evidence which lends credence to this theory is anything but sparse. Shakespeare married Anne Hathaway and produced three children before moving semi-permanently to London. Anecdotes from some of Shakespeare's contemporaries describe several extra-marital affairs of the playwright's as well, specifically with women of "common stock" or "base heritage," perhaps alluding to the fact that Shakespeare was a commoner himself and did not attempt to pursue women above his station. The sexually explicit sonnets dedicated to the Dark Lady would certainly also be evidence of his preference for and attraction to women.

On the other hand, far more of Shakespeare's sonnets are dedicated to the explicit physical beauty of and the poet's desire for a young man. While the physical act of sex would not have been explicitly stated in this series, there are numerous erotic puns littered through the collection, and the poet utilized monikers and words denoting romantic affection often. In many of the Fair Youth poems, the narrator laments sleepless nights, physical pangs of longing, and jealousy toward others who warrant the Fair Youth's attention.

More recent scholars have also criticized heavily older published editions of the sonnets, as well as analysis of them, based on the social and political biases that may have existed in their respective time periods. Homosexuality was not decriminalized in the United Kingdom until 1967. The most visible of Shakespearean scholars from the eighteenth through the twentieth centuries were Englishmen themselves, and to suggest that Shakespeare, their national treasure, could have had sexual relations with another man, would have been repugnant to many. There may have been some academics and historians in these periods who were open to the idea of (or at least not opposed to) Shakespeare's attraction to men, but to even write about it or suggest it would have put these scholars under much legal scrutiny. The safe analysis in the political climate of the age would have been to eschew any possible suggestion of Shakespeare being a "sodomite."

Regardless of who he may have loved or how he loved them, Shakespeare's sonnets had a major impact on poetic form for future generations. His collection of sonnets is considered the foundation for modern love poetry. He would freely associate and express new ideas on gender roles, make political commentary, write explicitly about sex and physical desire, and at times even debase the very idea of love at all. In yet another written form, Shakespeare set a new standard by casting off and ignoring typical writing conventions of the period, and blazed a new trail so that future writers could experiment in his wake.

Chapter Eight

The Death of William Shakespeare

"Life's but a walking shadow, a poor player
That struts and frets his hour upon the stage
And then is heard no more."

—William Shakespeare, Macbeth

After 1606, Shakespeare slowed down considerably. Though he did not stop writing until 1613, the plays he penned in his final years were collaborations with other playwrights, most notably John Fletcher. Fletcher would succeed Shakespeare as The King's Men's resident playwright, despite his unremarkable career as a solo writer. Shakespeare spent a majority of his time in his final decade in Stratford, which may have been due to the ongoing and sporadic outbreaks of bubonic plague that would strike London between 1603 and 1610. Minor recurrences of the illness would cause public spaces, including theatres, to shut down on short notice for unspecified amounts of time. In the seven-year period of these outbreaks, the Globe was closed for many months, which would have meant much less active work for Shakespeare and his troupe.

There exist records of a few of Shakespeare's brief return trips to London in his final years. In 1612 he was called as a witness in a legal case regarding a marriage settlement, while in 1613 he bought a gatehouse near Blackfriars Theatre, where The King's Men would perform in the winter months. In 1614, he would enter London as a companion of his son-in-law John Hall, a doctor who may have had business in the city's center.

Shakespeare endured some scandalous family drama in the final months of his life. His eldest daughter Susanna had married Doctor John Hall in 1607 and had given birth to daughter Elizabeth in 1608. Shakespeare was pleased with the match, enough so that Susanna and her husband were named the primary beneficiaries in the will he crafted only a month before his death. Susanna's place as the main benefactor, however, may have been due to the shameful events surrounding his other child.

Shakespeare's younger daughter Judith married Thomas Quiney, a vintner, only two months before her father's death. Within a month, Quiney was found guilty in court of fathering an illegitimate child which was stillborn to a woman who had also died in childbirth. It was highly likely that Judith was well aware of this and married Quiney anyway, hoping the fact would not come to light. The couple was excommunicated for some months, and the scandal would have brought immense shame on Shakespeare's family and their reputation.

It was during this very public drama that Shakespeare hastily amended his will, leaving nearly everything to Susanna and her husband. Judith was granted a sum equivalent to £20,000, but detailed stipulations were laid out to avoid Thomas Quiney having any access to the money, inheriting any of Shakespeare's property holdings, or having access to any part of the Shakespeare family estate.

William Shakespeare died suddenly on April 23, 1616. There is no evidence that he was in poor or declining health—in fact, the new will he had signed only a month prior had described him as being "in perfect health." No source contemporary with Shakespeare gives an explanation of circumstances or events that may have precipitated his death, such as illness or injury. Two days later, he was laid to rest at Holy Trinity Church in Stratford-upon-Avon, with an epitaph that curses anyone who dares disturb his grave. A large funerary monument was erected in Stratford in 1623 to commemorate his life and his achievements and the pride he had brought the community with his success.

Shakespeare's grand-daughter Elizabeth, the first child of Susanna and John Hall, never had children. Judith Quiney gave birth to three children but outlived them all. Shakespeare's direct line ended with his children but is immortalized in his writing and his legacy.

Chapter Nine

Legacy

"We know what we are, but know not what we may be."

—William Shakespeare, Hamlet

The legacy that William Shakespeare left behind is seen on stages across the world and throughout literature to this day. There exists no single play within Shakespeare's body of work that demarcates the shift from conventional Elizabethan theatrical styles into the freer poetic and story-driven style he wrote in his more mature years. Instead, his evolution can be charted as a continuously branching line throughout his entire career, even up to his final work.

In his first experiments, he broke away from the stilted and stylized language that was normal for the time, instead opting to build his skill in the use of blank verse. Upon mastering the so-called iambic pentameter in which he frequently wrote, he began to play with the traditional flow of that style. While *Romeo and Juliet* and *Hamlet* are both written in blank verse, *Hamlet* contains many syntactical devices that can make the language drive with hard force or flow with gentle grace, interrupting or adding weight to a rigid poetic form. Within *Hamlet*, Shakespeare begins to experiment with the use of soliloquy (when a character speaks his or her thoughts out loud). Soliloquies were typically used in theatre as an opportunity for a character to explain plot points to the audience to drive the action forward. Shakespeare, however, uses Hamlet's lonely speeches as a chance to explore the human psychological condition.

He would master the use of soliloquy as a form of character analysis in *Othello*, allowing villain Iago to converse directly with the audience and defend his traitorous actions. For the first time in theatre, the audience may have felt uneasiness with how simply the villain could make his case and ingratiate himself to their hearts.

In some of Shakespeare's final plays, *Macbeth* being the most notable example, he finds a perfect balance in variation on sentence length and flow, mixing in metaphors that are at once violent and beautiful, using the grammar of the poetic form to add depth to his characters. He could expertly take stories, histories, and themes that would be well known to audiences and re-shape them to create interest in particulars of such common stories which may have been glossed over in the past. His ability to draw the audience's attention to new centers of interest creates plays with themes that are timeless.

Shakespeare's use of language and meter allows his plays to be translated into nearly every language without losing meaning or the aural beauty of the poetry. Characters were given the opportunity to evolve organically within the writing, allowing actors centuries later to form new interpretations of fictional people who were first put on stage over 400 years ago.

This lifelong perfection of the writing craft set the foundation for writers and artists of all kinds in the centuries that followed. The Romantic period, a massive artistic movement that saw its height between 1800 and 1850, made huge attempts to bring Shakespeare's work back to the forefront of theatre, art, music, and literature. While the movers and shakers of the Romantic era failed to bring Shakespeare back into mainstream popular culture, the influence of his work can be seen in the biggest products of the Romantic Movement. One need only name a few of these figures to see the connection between Shakespeare and the likes of Jane Austen, Henry David Thoreau, William Wordsworth, Edgar Allen Poe, and the trio of John Keats and Mary and Percy Shelley.

In the 400 years since Shakespeare's life, scholars have definitively named 20,000 pieces of music that have been composed in response to his original work. Pre-Raphaelite painters took much of their inspiration from the idyllic scenery in Shakespeare's comedies, as well as the heartfelt emotion in his tragedies. Twentieth-century psychoanalyst Sigmund Freud, long considered the father of modern psychology, used Shakespeare's character studies (and particularly that of Hamlet) to create his insights into the human mind.

Even today, we see Shakespeare's body of work being viewed through new lenses and filters of the modern world. His ability to create relatable characters has drawn feminist movements to use his work to explore and advance new ideas, allowed African-American communities to explore their sense of belonging, and most recently has allowed queer communities to experiment with new theatrical styles through the structure of period drama. His legacy will continue to grow and evolve much as he did throughout his life, allowing human beings from every background and time in history to connect to each other through the binding agent of his plays.

Conclusion

William Shakespeare began his life at a turning point in English history. The Elizabethan Age was in its golden years, but political and religious conflicts throughout Europe meant change would come swiftly whether London was ready or not. Afforded the benefits of being one of the first members of the middle class, Shakespeare had opportunities in early education that he may not have been lucky enough to take advantage of otherwise.

To this day, debates rage about numerous aspects of Shakespeare's life, including his religion, his political views, and even his sexuality. His timeless themes and messages unify people across social strata and even across the span of centuries, and when looking at his enduring legacy he becomes a mythical legend quite like King Arthur—mysterious, magically gifted, carrying the torch of English values, history, and ingenuity into the modern world.

William Shakespeare's work endures not because of the quantity of work he produced, nor due to any particularly poignant political or religious message that informs us of the time in which he lived. His writing stood the test of time and transcended the products of his peers because he was the first to write about the collective human experience. We care about the beautiful language, the unique metaphors, and the exciting plots, to be sure, but it is what lies beneath that keeps us engaged as human beings. We do not have to be princes to feel the indecision of Hamlet; we do not have to lead armies to feel the ambition of Macbeth or the jealousy and insecurity of Othello. We want Romeo and Juliet to be together; we want to warn Julius Caesar of the conspiracy against him, or even perhaps feel the deep insidious urge to join in on the plot. William Shakespeare wrote about the heart of what it is to be a human and will endure as a pioneer of our exploration and self-reflection into the endless annals of time.

Made in the USA
Middletown, DE
25 November 2023

43500449R00029